Greece Travel Guide

51 Amazing Things to Do in Greece

By 51 Amazing Things

Contents

In this guide, you will know more about 51 different places and experiences that should be on your travel itinerary.

- Know more about ancient antiquity architectural and archaeological treasures like The Acropolis and The Theater of Epidaurus.

- Know more about amazing tourist attractions before visiting them. Know the histories of post-Roman structures like Meteora in Thessaly and the Little Metropolis Church in Athens.

- Get to know the best beaches in Greece. As they are scattered all over the country, it's good to know which island to go to and experience one or more of Greece's pristine beaches.

- Know where to get the best dining and nightclub experience. After all, Greece is not just about museums, archaeological wonders, and beaches.

- Experience Greece's history through its museums. Even the islands themselves can be considered as museums, as they give visitors a glimpse into their past.
- Know more about some of Greece's natural wonders. You can explore the caves, swim in the majestic lakes, or walk through forests and sand dunes.

Introduction

Greece is not only known for its Classical buildings, but it's also known for its amazing food, landscape, beaches, natural wonders, islands, museums, and World Heritage sites. Moreover, Greece is a beautiful country characterized by long sandy beaches, thousands of islands, fantastic weather and mountainous landscapes.

Greece is a favorite tourism destination for Europeans and many other nationalities around the world. According to the National Statistical Service of Greece, the country ranks 15th in the world rating for tourism destinations. Greece gets 15 million visitors annually, after countries like Great Britain, Spain, China, and the United States.

Why Greece? The country is popular for its ancient history and pristine beaches, not to mention the myriad of activities that one can do in the country. While this book mentions 51 amazing locations and activities to do in Greece, there are thousands of places to go to and activities to experience in the country's 1,400 islands (169 inhabited) and islets.

Greece is not only a country for ancient history, but it's also a cosmopolitan country that sees international visitors enjoying the country's vibrant nightlife and dining scene. You can also visit museums, and indulge in the country's prehistoric and modern history. You can also get to experience the country's natural wonders like kayaking in the caves or trekking the sand dunes.

There's a myriad of things to do in Greece, and the book mentions just 51, to begin with. Experience Greece. When you go back to your home country, you will be filled with memories of Greece.

Chapter 1: Amazing Antiquities

1. The Acropolis, Athens

Your Athens vacation would not be complete without a trip to the Acropolis. Athens' most defining attraction is an ancient citadel that consists of several temples built around 5th century BCE. Some of the Acropolis' most important structures include the Propylaea, the Temple of Athena Nike, and the Erechtheion. However, the citadel's most architecturally important building is the Parthenon, a Classical temple built to honor the patron of ancient Athens – the goddess Athena.

The Acropolis is currently undergoing massive restoration work. The Temple of Athena Nike was fully restored in 2010. The Propylaea's floor and roof are partially restored. Destroyed during the 17th century Venetian bombardment, the colonnades of the Parthenon were restored, and erroneously assembled columns are now properly placed.

Reaching the Acropolis is relatively easy, and the Akropoli Metro Station is near the Acropolis' eastern entrance. There's a €20 entrance fee for the Acropolis, and be prepared for a lot of uphill climbing. You can also enter through the south and west entrances, which are bordered by large avenues lined with restaurants and cafes.

The best times to go up the citadel are late winter or spring when you can see wildflowers and grass growing amid the marble. You can go to the Acropolis on your own, or you can join tour groups with licensed guides. Guided tours can cost about EUR50 and above. You can spend around four hours touring both the Acropolis and the Athenian Agora.

2. The Athenian Agora, Athens

Established during the 6th century BCE, the Athenian Agora is located beneath the Acropolis' northern slope. The marketplace was the ancient city's economic center, where the influence, reach, and wealth of classical Athens was apparent with the wide array of goods – ranging from precious Levant dyes to Black Sea wheat – from the port of Piraeus.

However, what made the Agora glorious was the daily peddling and trading of ideas. The Agora was the hangout spot and meeting place for Athenians, wherein elected politicians met to discuss state affairs. Here, ordinary citizens met with friends and watched various performances, and noblemen gathered to do business. Philosophers also regaled their audience with their brand of wisdom.

The Agora's architectural layout revolved around the Panathenaic Way, which ran through the ancient city center to the city's main gate, the Dipylon. The Panathenaic Way also was the travel route for the Panathenaic festival, held every four years to honor the goddess, Athena. The Agora also contained the Temple of Hephaestus, which is still well-preserved. The Agora also formerly accommodated various temples and stoas – covered porticos for public use.

The Agora has two entrances: the south entrance is along the Adrianou road, while the north entrance is approached from the Acropolis. While you can join tour groups, you can also tour the Agora with your own intimate group. Entrance fee is EUR8. Touring the Agora doesn't entail steep climbing, but it's always a good idea to wear comfortable shoes. A tour guide or an excellent guide book can help a lot.

3. Dion Archaeological Park, Dion

The Dion Archaeological Park, which is located in the vicinity of Mount Olympus, is a half-ancient city and half-swamp that is a playground for naturalists and archaeologists alike. The ancient city of Dion once hosted notables like Alexander the Great. However, its ponds and lush greenery are currently home to critters like frogs, butterflies, birds, fish, spiders, turtles, and weasels.

The archaeological site features the ruins of a Roman temple and a Greek temple. There is also a partially-preserved Roman bath complex. The other side of the site features private villas, including the Villa of Dionysus. The site also accommodated sanctuaries to Zeus, Demeter, Asclepius, and the Egyptian goddess Isis.

The city of Dion used to be the sacred seat for Zeus. Throughout the centuries, it became a Roman colony, and a Christian-era bishopric before people started to abandon the place. The site was rediscovered in the 19th and 20th centuries, and its monuments have been restored. As they have been left in their original state, visitors may feel as if they are in a forgotten civilization.

The onsite Dion Archaeological Museum houses a collection of artifacts from the ruins. The site is outside the modern town of Dion, which is off the E75 highway that runs between Thessaloniki and Larissa. The Dion Archaeological Park opens daily from 8 am to 7 pm and closes at 3 pm from November to March. The museum opens Tuesdays to Sundays from 8 am to 7 pm, and closes at 3 pm from November to March.

4. Mycenae, Argolis

The ancient city of Mycenae was once the major power in Helladic Greece and the Bronze Age, controlling most of the south and trading with Egypt and Crete. Mycenae is the home of mythological and literary figures like Perseus and the House of Atreus. It was also home to Agamemnon.

Excavations in the ancient city began in 1874 and unearthed shaft graves that contained goods like jewels, weapons, and gold death masks. The site's famed features are the tholoi or beehive tombs, which marked a shift in burial practices.

Mycenae also has slippery stone steps that lead to an ancient cistern's remnants. The cistern, which drew water from a nearby spring, gave Mycenaean citizens access to water even when outside forces attacked the city.

If you are staying in Athens or nearby cities, coach tours are the best ways to reach Mycenae. They offer full day tours and even stop at the Theater of Epidaurus. You can also take the Athens-Napflio bus, which stops at the village of Fihtio. The buses stop in both Fihtio and Mycenae. You can even stay in one of the village's small hotels.

Summer is usually the best time to visit Mycenae. While tourism is restricted to the archaeological area, there are efforts to use the region as an agriculture destination.

5. The Oracle of Delphi, Phocis

Delphi, for the ancient Greeks, was the world's center. Ancient Greeks also united here to worship Apollo. Delphi was also known for its mysterious sanctuary, where Pythia – the priestess of Apollo – made her prophecies.

Pythia perched upon a chasm, which was believed to emit fumes that are believed to be hallucinogenic. The priestess deeply breathed and went into semi-consciousness, with her prophecies often frantic and opaque. The priestess did her prophecies in the Oracle of Delphi, which was the ancient Greeks' most feared, most famous window into the gods' will. The Oracle of Delphi lay in a hillside cavern underneath Apollo's temple.

The temple's ruins sit on the Mount Parnassus slopes. In 390 CE, Emperor Theodosius I destroyed the temple to eliminate pagan beliefs. There are still traces of the Oracle. However, you may find the site eerie. You can nearly hear the ghosts of Alexander, Nero, and Croesus. The mist that clings to the hills adds to the place's enchanting quality.

From Athens, you can join day tours that can cost from €80 to €100, and a bus journey from the capital takes 3 hours. A one-way bus fare costs €16.40. It's relatively easy to get around Delphi, and walking is the only way to explore the haunting attraction. The site and museum are also within walking distance from civilization, but taxis are available readily.

6. Palace of Knossos, Heraklion, Crete

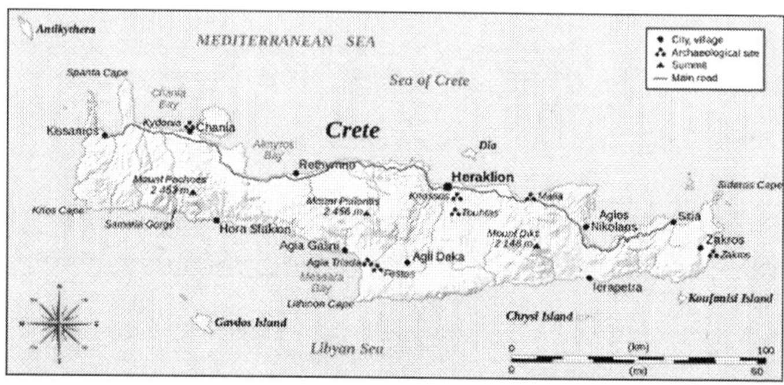

The ruins of Knossos near the modern city of Heraklion comprise King Minos' legendary Palace of Knossos, which was razed by fire around 1450 BCE. The town was deserted and was lost to time. The palace is the subject of ancient Greek lore, with the palace's center containing the mythical Minotaur's labyrinth. The palace is also connected to the story of Icarus and Daedalus.

Arthur Evans, a British archaeologist, began excavations at the site beginning 1900. Over a quarter of a century, he unearthed the ruins of a palace, believed to be the Palace of Knossos.

Excavations revealed Knossos was inhabited from the Neolithic Age (7000 to 3000 BCE) to the Roman times. Over a million visitors flock to Knossos each year.

The Palace of Knossos is 5 kilometers away from Heraklion. The site and the Heraklion Archaeological Museum are open daily during the winters from 8:30 am to 3 pm. In the summers, the sites open from 8 am to 7:30 pm. Tickets to the palace cost EUR16.

7. Samothrace Temple Complex, Paleopoli

This is not your average tourist attraction, as it's not often visited, is on an 180 square meter island, and can only be accessed by ferry. The island of Samothrace is home to Mt. Phengari, one of the Aegean's highest mountains. The island's Pan-Hellenic temple complex, which is also called the Samothrace Sanctuary of the Great

Gods, is located on the island's northeastern portion.

The Great Mother's (Mother of the Gods or Meter Theon Idaia) was central to the worship, and certain historical figures are believed to have been initiated into it. These figures included Phillip II of Macedonia, Herodotus, and Lysander, among many others. The sanctuary also hosted Roman emperors like Hadrian. However, the Fall of Rome caused the complex to be discontinued as a place of worship.

Excavations in the 1700s and 1800s led to the discovery of the Nike of Samothrace (Victory of Samothrace) statue. The statue now is housed in the Louvre Museum, at the Daru staircase's head. The statue's replica stands at a Samothrace archaeological museum.

The island of Samothrace itself is perfect for rural retreats, as it doesn't have an extensive tourist infrastructure. The island, however, comes alive during the yearly music festival.

To go to Samothrace, you can ride a ferry (with services operated by Saos Ferries) from Alexandroupolis. Buses also connect to various parts of the island. When going to the temple complex from Kamariotissa, take the route going to Therma.

8. Theater of Epidaurus, Peloponnesus

The Theater of Epidaurus is considered one of the best preserved Greek ancient theaters in terms of fine structure and perfect acoustics. The theater was built in the 4th century BCE. The theater originally had 34 rows of seats, which were divided into 34 blocks by walkways and stairs. The theater is set near the sanctuary of the Greek god of healing Asclepius.

The theater is remarkable in the sense that 15,000 spectators can perfectly hear the actors. The theater was built by Polycleitus on a mountainside, with the theater overlooking Asclepius's sanctuary. The conclave's highest distance is 58 meters, while the stage's diameter is 20 meters.

Beginning in 1954, the Athens Epidaurus Festival is held each summer with modern plays and ancient dramas. The festival, throughout the years, has hosted both foreign and Greek artists.

The Theater of Epidaurus is two hours away from Athens and is a half-hour trip away by car from the town of Nafplio. When driving from Nafplio, pass through Lygourio and head towards Sanctuary of Asclepius archaeological site. There are also numerous day and coach trips organized from Athens. Nearby sites to visit include Corinth, Nafplio, and Mycenae.

However, there are certain restrictions upon reaching the theater, which has an entrance fee of €6. The most important of them is the indiscriminate throwing of chewing gum, which can irreparably damage the theater.

Chapter 2: Amazing Attractions

9. The Gennadius Library, Athens

Also known as the Gennadeion, the Gennadius Library is set within the premises of the American School of Classical Studies in Athens. The Gennadeion, which was designed by W. Stuart Thompson and John Van Pelt, mostly deals with post-classical materials, including more than 120,000 items pertaining to modern Greece and its neighboring countries. In 1926, the Gennadeion was opened to the public, after Joannes Gennadius – in 1922 – donated 26,000 documents and volumes.

Gennadius – a serious collector and bibliophile – sought to highlight the Greek cultural greatness between modern and ancient times by promoting Greek artists and writers' work. Some of the collections include original works by Odysseas Elytis, George Seferis, and Heinrich Schliemann.

Aside from literature, the Gennadeion's non-circulating collection includes watercolors, scrapbooks, archaeological reports, maps, works of art, rare books, and travelogues, making the Gennadeion a diverse and vast resource for modern Mediterranean history and culture. The Gennadius Library also organizes cultural events like lectures, concerts, and exhibits.

The library is designed with an imposing white-marbled entrance and characterized by Ionic columns. It's also set within a well-kept, large garden with Mediterranean flora. The Gennadius Library is set in Central Athens with its location on 61 Souidias Street. It can be reached via the Metro Blue Line, and the nearest station is the Evangelismos Station.

10. Holy Mount of Athos, Agion Oros

The Holy Mount of Athos, which is an autonomous theocratic society within Greece's borders, is directly governed by the Universal Patriarch of Constantinople. Mount Athos' oldest monasteries date back to the 900s. The region, however, only became relevant during the Byzantine Empire's latter years and at the start of the Ottoman rule.

To escape the Ottoman armies and the marauders, Christian monks sought refuge in Mount Athos' dense forests and steep cliffs. The community quickly grew and became one of the European Orthodoxy's most important centers. It became a beacon for spiritual enlightenment seekers, even from far away Georgia and Russia. After the decline of communism, Mount Athos experienced a population resurgence with Eastern European migrants coming in.

The current population is about 2,200 inhabitants, and Mount Athos houses 20 monasteries strewn over a 60 kilometer-long peninsula. The region's administrative center is Karyes. Tourist visits are tightly monitored. An interesting rule is that women are banned from Mount Athos, and such prohibition has been in place for over 1,000 years. According to monks, the ban is born out of the human spirit's weakness.

Entry to Mount Athos is via ferry boat from either the port of Ierrisos (for east coast monasteries) or Ouranoupoli's port (for west coast monasteries). Before leaving the respective ports, visitors must have been handed a diamonitirion – a type of visa. Once the pilgrim is issued the pass, he can contact the monastery he wishes to stay in.

11. Little Metropolis Church, Athens

Little Metropolis Church (Mikri Mitropoli) is set right next to the Metropolitan Cathedral of Athens (Megali Mitropoli). Despite its small 20 feet x 40 feet size, this church should not be discounted as it is rich in history.

The church creation's purported dates widely vary, and scholars argue that it's anywhere between the 8th and 15th centuries. The church was built over the ruins of a temple to the patron of childbirth, the goddess Eileithyia. During its time, the church was able to accommodate Athens' still-small population.

The church was built from repurposed building materials, especially marble blocks from pagan temples. Such a move made sense. As using temple marble was convenient and cheap, it also eliminated from public records the old heathen religious artifacts.

The common practice is called 'spolia,' and the process of 'baptizing' or 'sphragis' of the pagan objects was simply carving a cross on the object. Nearly all of the church's blocks containing images have small crosses etched into them despite the depiction of ancient Roman and Greek gods.

When going to the church, it's best to go on foot. The church is only a short distance from the National Gardens and certain major Athenian ruins. Little Metropolis Church is open from dawn to dusk, and entrance to the church is free.

12. Meteora, Thessaly

Meteora is Greece's second most important monastery complex. However, what makes Meteora even more awe-inspiring is that the monastery is perched atop a series of visually stunning geological wonders. Water, harsh temperatures, and the wind have resulted in the formation of massive sandstone pillars – some of them rising to hundreds of meters.

The monastery started to flourish after the Ottoman conquest in 1453. During the time, Orthodox monks escaped persecution and sought refuge in remote locations. One of them is Meteora.

To originally access Meteora, one had to be dragged with a large net or had to climb ladders that were tied together. Nowadays, one can now use the steps carved into the rock to reach the monastery complex. Another access is a bridge from a neighboring plateau. Of the six existing monasteries in the complex, Great Meteora is the one often visited by pilgrims and is the largest.

When visiting Meteora, visitors should wear proper attire: pants and long sleeves for men and below-knee length skirts for women. You can get into Meteora by bus and train, with buses to and from Athens and Delphi. Trikala Bus Company sets up bus trips to Meteora from various Greek cities.

You can ride a train from Athens at the Larissa station, and you can get the schedules from the TrainOSE website. The ride is about 4 ½ to 5 hours long. The taxi fare from the train station to the monasteries can cost about EUR40.

13. Pittaki Street, Athens

Pittaki Street in Athens – before 2012 – was an often-avoided industrial alleyway, and was sometimes referred to as a public toilet. The alley, which is in the Psyrri neighborhood, used be lined with industrial sites and warehouses. To make the alleyway usable again, lighting studio Beforelight and non-profit Imagine the City collected unused light fixtures from around the city to light up the little pathway.

Athenians contributed various lights to reflect Athens' multicultural identity: Chinese paper lanterns, Midcentury metal lamps, stained glass lamps, the 1940s fringed and floral lampshades, and Ikea lamps. Volunteers then used soft pastels to paint the alley with homey scenes of living rooms and kitchen furniture.

Since 2012, Pittaki Street has become a cheerful Psyrri hub. The street now sees people regularly walking through it, and pose for photographs. Events are also staged here. Thanks to the project, Pittaki Street has become a tourist and commercial attraction.

14. Syntagma Square Metro Station

When you step inside the Syntagma Square Metro Station, you would feel that you are in an antiquities museum or at an excavation site. In an extraordinary move, archaeologists collaborated with Metro engineers on the project. Syntagma Square is the site of the city's first subway, as well as the city's largest archaeological excavation.

The engineers and archaeologists uncovered an astounding 30,000 to 50,000 artifacts, and the result is a combination of a broader knowledge of the city's history and a Metro station doubling as a museum.

The Syntagma Square area is near ancient cemeteries that have been around since the 11th century BCE. Thus, the station displays funerary goods and ancient Greek plumbing artifacts. At the station, the substrata beneath the city is exhibited behind a glass wall.

One can see layers of civilization from the Byzantine, Roman, ancient Greek, and prehistoric times, including the open grave of an original ancient necropolis. The Syntagma Square Metro Station is the stop nearest to the Greek Parliament.

15. Windmills of Lasithi Plateau, Crete

The Windmills of Lasithi Plateau have the distinction of belonging to history's first wind park. The plateau is home to a small rural enclave that had relied on over 10,000 identical windmills for irrigation.

Since 600 BCE, the plateau had been drawing settlers with only occasional harsh climate and fertile soil. The high water table that contributes to the soil's fertility, however, makes tilling the land tricky because of water saturation. During winter, run-off from rain would cause flooding and destroy the harvest. Ditches were dug to partially solve the problem.

During the 20th century, the windmills started to pop up to facilitate proper irrigation. Most of the windmills had white cloth sails and stone structures. Around 10,000 windmills popped up throughout the area, using the wind to pump water to the valley's fields. Together with the dug ditches, crop production became more viable.

Nowadays, there are only 5,000 windmills standing, and the plateau's residents have adopted modern irrigation methods. The remaining windmills symbolized simpler times, and lend the Lasithi Plateau a unique quality. There is also a renewed interest in the windmills' restoration, bringing back the old beauty of Lasithi Plateau.

Buses are the usual way to see the Windmills of Lasithi Plateau. There are bus stations in Agios Nikolaos, Ierapetra, and Sitia. There are also taxi services in the area.

Chapter 3: Amazing Beaches

16. Elafonisi, Crete

Elafonisi Beach lies on Crete's southwestern side and around 75 kilometers from Chania. The magical beach consists of a small islet pink and white sandy beaches. Elafonisi Beach is also near the main beach, which is busy during summers.

You can reach Elafonisi on foot as the waters are shallow. At times, your toes might never get wet. The beach is, therefore, excellent for families having small children. Its root word ‘elafi’ is Greek for deer as, years ago, people found they can get to the islet barefoot – much like the way a deer walks. As a Natura 2000 protected area, Elafonisi Beach is a flat parcel of land with random vegetation against the Cretan mountains’ stark bareness.

The majority of the action happens between the island and the mainland. It may not be an ideal place for quality time with your significant other or a place to swim. Rather, the beach is more suited for its warm, shallow water that’s great for children practicing their swimming skills. The nearly mile-long Elafonisi Beach has a number of small coves, interesting rock formations, and sandy beaches. It’s also a home for 110 species of flora.

About 5 kilometers north of Elafonisi Beach is the Chrysoskalitisa monastery, which resembles a forest due to its higher altitude location. Legend says the monastery staircase's last step is made of gold, but only true believers in God can see it.

17. Fragos (Simos), Elafonisos

The island of Elafonisos – between the Peloponnese and Kythira – is well known for its beaches. The 19 square kilometer island lies off the Vatika and the coast of Cape Malea. As its Peloponnese's largest island, Elafonisos is its own municipality.

Tourism season in Elafonisos is from May to September, with the high season in July and August. The island is known for its sandy, white beaches. Its crystal-clear waters has a unique emerald hue. One of the well-known beaches is Fragos, which is one of two beaches that comprise Simos Beach.

Simos' twin beach system – Fragos and Sarakiniko – is perhaps the best known beach in Peloponnese. Its majestic sand dunes host a sensitive yet dynamic flora ecosystem. The sand in

August is full of the endangered sand lily plants (Pancratium maritimum). Other species include Ammophila (ammophila arenara) and Agatha (Eryngium maritimum).

From the mainland, you can enter Elafonisos via ferry. During the high season, there are frequent trips – normally hourly or twice an hour. There is also a connection between Neapolis and Elafonisos during peak season. You may also enter through the Kythira airport from the mainland, and then transfer to Elafonisos through the Neapolis ferry.

18. Kolymbithres, Paros

The rock formations are part of the reason why Kolymbithres Beach in Paros, which is part of the Cycladic Islands, is a favorite spot for locals and tourists. It's impressive and distinct white rock formations make Kolymbithres Beach a unique diving spot.

Located in Naoussa Bay, the Kolymbithres Beach has its own ethereal, otherworldly quality. Sea and wind have sculpted the smooth-shaped granite rocks over time. The rock formations are now one of Paros' go-to destinations. The area also has numerous tiny coves. Kolymbithres Beach is also a photographers' delight due to its dry-land colorful shrubs, clear waters, and unique rock formations.

You can never run out of things to do in Kolymbithres Beach. You can explore the majestic rock formations, lounge on a chair by the sand, and swim among fish. There's a watersport shack that offers water skis, kayaks, and other equipment. Along the road going to the beach, there are a few taverns and beach bars.

Kolymbithres Beach is accessible by private transportation, local bus, and small fishing boats (caiques). The caiques regularly depart from Naoussa's port. If you are bringing your own transportation, you can park at the space above the beach.

19. Lia, Mykonos

Lia Beach in Mykonos may be in one of the island's remotest parts, but it offers the tranquility that many beaches don't offer. The beach is situated about 14 kilometers from Chora Mykonos in the island's southern part. Chora is near Kalafatis.

Shielded by the summer winds, the sandy bay's deep clear waters are an excellent choice for those who wish to relax on a sun bed under an umbrella comfortably. Lia Beach is perfect for the more peace-loving, solitary individuals. The beach area has a large coffee shop and a fish tavern.

The well-organized Lia Beach has sundecks, colorful umbrellas, and many other useful amenities. The white sand and blue waters create the perfect swimmer's paradise combination. Rocks surround the beach, which can also be an excellent place for snorkeling and diving. You can easily access the beach if you pass through or depart from the village of Ano Mera and then follow the road signs.

Lia Beach's surrounding hills are predominantly bare, and the natural environment gives you a sense of absolute freedom.

The island of Mykonos, which is part of the Cyclades, can be accessed from the mainland towns of Piraeus and Rafina via high-speed catamaran and ferries. Mykonos can also be reached by plane as it has an airport 4 kilometers away from the Chora. Aegean Airlines and Olympic Air provide daily flights from Athens.

20. Navagio Beach, Zakynthos

Also known as 'Smuggler's Cove' and 'Shipwreck Beach,' Navagio Beach is known for the crumbling remnants of a smuggler's shipwreck. In 1983, the shipping vessel Panagiotis crashed on the pristine shore. Reports say the ship was smuggling booze, cigarettes, and possibly humans when the authorities followed the ship's trail through bad weather, and right into the Navagio Beach cove. Since the crash, the ship's hull just sat on the shore, slowly disintegrating.

The crash site soon saw the influx of vacationers who are drawn by the decaying ship's siren song. An extra bonus for these vacationers is the untouched and pristine beach with its clear waters. As the ship's bulkhead slowly rusts, the hull seemingly sinks into the sands. Most of the vessel is still visible, though.

The beach nowadays continues to be a popular tourist draw for people looking for quiet adventure. During peak times, however, the beach can get crowded – all thanks to the infamous shipwreck.

As a cove encloses Navagio Beach, the only way to reach it is from the sea. Most Zakynthos tour operators run day trips to the beach. From the Greek mainland, you can reach Zakynthos by plane via Athens. By ship, you can reach Zakynthos from Kyllini on the mainland.

21. Paleochori, Milos

Milos is the Cyclades group's south-westernmost island. The island is famed for the Venus de Milo and other statues representing Apollo, Poseidon, and Asclepius. Milos is also known for its pristine beaches, one of them being Paleochori. The area is a party beach that is surrounded by colorful volcanic rocks.

Paleochori Beach is characterized by its pebbled – not sandy – beach. While there is sand in some patches, most of the beach is covered with smooth pebbles with various colors like orange, crystal white, brown, and red. Rock formations divide the beach into a western and eastern part, and the beach's two sides are connected via a narrow path.

When you swim, you may notice a light sulfurous odor. At times, the odor can be intense. The odor comes from underwater sulfur springs, which protrudes slightly from the seabed like mini volcano craters and can be noticed a few meters from the shore.

The sulfur springs can warm up the seawater slightly, which can be pleasant for swimmers. If you wish to admire the sulfur springs up close, you may want to dive in. Just don't forget your snorkel and goggles.

Paleochori Beach is located in southern Milos and can be accessed easily from the road. From Milos's port, Adamas, the beach is only 10 to 15 minutes away by car. Local buses also pass through Paleochori.

22. Sarakiniko, Milos

Each of the islands of Milos's beaches are unique, and one of the most distinct beaches on the island is Sarakiniko Beach, which is named after Saracen pirates. Located on the island's northeastern shore, Sarakiniko is characterized by the gray-white volcanic rock that has been shaped by the north winds into fantastic shapes. The area has often been compared to a lunar landscape. Additionally, Sarakiniko Beach is one of the Aegean's most-photographed landscapes.

The beach is quite small and can be crowded with swimmers during the peak season. However, there's always a reason not to miss this beach. It's nestled between almost-polished white cliffs and rocks presumably originating from calcium materials. As you walk through the rocks, you may feel that you are on the moon.

A few meters off the shore is a five meter-high rock for diving aficionados. The beach waters are quite shallow until you reach the bay's entrance. The beach is perfect for families with children. It's also a treat to visit Sarakiniko at night, especially during the full moon, as the white rocks vividly reflect the moonlight.

Sarakiniko Beach is close to the port of Adamas, and you can access the beach easily by car. Just follow the signs, and you will arrive at a parking lot. From there, you can walk along 200 meters of a white pathway until you reach the scenic beach. Close to Sarakiniko is a wrecked ship near the shore. The attraction's two parts are jutting out of the sea. The remnants of the ship are less than 100 meters from the shore.

Chapter 4: Amazing Dining and Nightlife

23. Holy Spirit Beach Bar, Varkiza, Athens

Within the Varkiza Resort in Athens, the Holy Spirit Beach Bar is not your average noisy bar. Its atmosphere is more fun with its colorful décor, surfboards, funky atmosphere, chill music, and exotic cocktails. The bar exists to add amazing sparkle to summer nights at Varkiza's main beach.

Holy Spirit Beach Bar is, even more, fun as it operates all day long, promising you sand, sun, and fun with cocktails like XL Margaritas. It's one such seaside location where you can get an exceptional collection of spirits. Some of the recommended cocktails include Fantastic Boyfriend and Blue Hawaiian.

Holy Spirit Beach Bar

Varkiza Resort

Varkiza, Athens

(+30) 6979 772191

24. Island Club & Restaurant, Varkiza, Athens

Island Club & Restaurant's amazing location is on the coastal road to Varkiza, Athens. Visiting celebrities and jet setters make sure to stop by Island during any of their travels to Greece. The vintage furniture integrates seamlessly with the place's contemporary design.

Island Restaurant is adjacent to the club and sits on a rock that overlooks the Aegean. Classic Mediterranean dishes include handmade pasta, meat, and fish. The restaurant's menu also includes Asian-fusion and sushi. The restaurant's cellar has over 150 labels of international and Greek wines, spirits, and champagnes.

For 20 years, the Island club is one of the most visited locations for people who seek style and quality. Frozen cocktails, dance, lounge music, and local and international visitors come together to create the ideal club atmosphere, every day, each week, and until the end of summer.

Island Club & Restaurant

27th klm Athinon Souniou

Athens, 16672

islandclubrestaurant.gr

(+30) 210 9653563

25. Loft Club, Heraklion, Crete

Loft Club, is located in the Heraklion city center, is situated on a Milatou street building. The bar and club are perfect for dancing nights that will instantaneously put you in the right mood. Moreover, the fun staff and great music, especially the Greek pop music (ellinadiko) let you enjoy the amazing night away.

At Loft Club, you get to experience amazing music and great parties. From Tuesdays to Saturdays, the club hosts different parties with shifting DJ sets each day. Loft Club opens all year round at 11:45 pm to 7:00 am from Tuesdays to Saturdays. During mid-summers, the club may be open for extra nights during the week.

Loft Club

Meramvelou Street & Idaiou Androu Street

Iraklio Old Town

Heraklion, Crete

(+30) 6945 979354

26. The Old Tavern of Psarras, Athens

Since the late 1800s, The Old Tavern of Psarras has been serving its patron's flavorful Greek cuisine. With its wooden tables arranged under a mulberry tree's shade, and with its accessibility to white-washed steps leading to the Acropolis, the atmosphere can't get any more magical. As the oldest Greek restaurant in Plaka, the Psarras tavern – each evening – lightens up each meal experience with live Greek music.

If you seek a traditional Greek atmosphere, try the kebab lamb, the clay pot lamb, or any of the fresh fish dishes. In Athens, with its abundant sunshine, seating in the Psarras tavern offers a majestic view of old and new Athens. The restaurant also provides total relaxation after a stroll through the Plaka area.

The Old Tavern of Psarras is housed in two Neo-Classical buildings, and the space between the two buildings – during the summer months – serves hungry locals and tourists. What's also to love about the tavern are its wooden floors and warm colors, with the old items collection and impressive fireplace beautifully blending in.

The Old Tavern of Psarras

16 Erechtheos & Erotokritou Streets

Plaka – Athens

http://www.psaras-taverna.gr/

info@psaras-taverna.gr

(+30) 210 3218734

27. Rakkan Bar Restaurant, Kifissia, Athens

Rakkan Bar Restaurant is not your average restaurant. Even its name, Rakkan, is Japanese for optimism. Simplicity characterizes the Japanese fusion restaurant, and its interiors acclaimed by design magazines around the world.

The 9,900 wooden cubes that partly make Rakkan famous can be likened to a reverse maquette. During summers, the outdoor area shines with its atrium decorated with dim lighting, comfortable sofas, and superb acoustics.

Rakkan's Chefs Naruse Fumiake and Giannis Simotas combine fusion and creative cuisine with recipes and techniques from Japan and Europe, creating a 'Euro-Oriental' approach.

Delightful menu items include the Raspberry Goat Cheese Salad with raspberry dressing, nuts, tomato jam, and chevre cheese; Black Cod Fish & Chips with Peruvian chips, Alaska cod, and broccoli mouse; and Black Angus Mini Buns Burgers with kimchi cabbage, ranchera sauce, steamed bread, and aged cheddar cheese.

Rakkan Bar Restaurant is also known for its cocktails menu, with items inspired by Japanese culture.

Rakkan Bar Restaurant

Kifisias Avenue 238-240

Kifissia, Athens

www.rakkanrestaurant.gr

E-mail info@rakkanrestaurant.com

(+30) 210 8087941

28. Spilia Sea Side Restaurant, Mykonos

Next to the Kalafatis Beach on Mykonos, within the Agia Anna cove, is a unique restaurant-bar that seems to be carved amid the rocks – Spilia Sea Side Restaurant. Because it blends seamlessly with the Aegean seaside landscape, Spilia is also one of Mykonos' most iconic hotspots.

Spilia's all-day menu features an authentic Mykonian-Mediterranean culinary experience. Fresh from the Aegean, you are served fresh fish and seafood that include mussels, oysters, crayfish, lobsters, and urchins. All these you can enjoy while gazing at the brilliant Aegean Sea.

Spilia is also the place to go if you want to enjoy an idyllic Mykonos meal. At the restaurant, you'll also get to see a beautiful international crowd. Aside from the fresh seafood, the restaurant is known for its lobster pasta. Aside from the superb Mediterranean seafood offerings, the friendly staff, idyllic ambiance, and music are reasons to dine at Spilia.

Spilia Sea Side Restaurant

Agia Anna Beach, Kalafatis

Ano Mera, 84600 Mykonos Island

spilia.seaside@gmail.com

Tel. (+30) 6949-449729

29. Varoulko Seaside Restaurant, Athens

Enjoy the best of Mediterranean seafood at Varoulko Seaside in Piraeus, within the Athens metropolitan area. As the brainchild of Chef Lefteris Lazarou, Varoulko's menu is inspired by the sea. Lazarou's constantly evolving menu is creative yet reminds of tradition. It's distinctly Greek and innovative.

At the Varoulko in Piraeus, you can sample a lunch with dishes like taramosalata (fish roe dip) with white roe, olive oil, and lemon, or the vinegar-marinated octopus (htapodi xydato). You can also enjoy a more elaborate menu and enjoy fish patties with a peppery sweet-and-sour sauce, or the cuttlefish with orange sauce and caramelized lentils.

What makes the food even more amazing is that you get to enjoy them in the spectacular maritime environment. You can indulge in the picturesque Mikrolimano marina view – especially at night. The affordable prices and impeccable service are some of the things that make you come back for more during your stay in Greece.

Varoulko Seaside Restaurant

Akti Koumoundourou 52

Mikrolimano, Piraeus

info@varoulko.gr

(+30) 210 5228400

Chapter 5: Amazing Islands and Old Towns

30. Akrotiri, Santorini

Nestled on the island of Santorini's southern tip is the Bronze Age settlement of Akrotiri, which enjoyed prosperity for many years before being wiped out by a massive volcanic eruption. The remains of the Minoan town are well-preserved, much like Pompeii's ruins.

During the 2nd millennium BCE, the volcano – Thera – erupted, causing the inhabitants of Akrotiri to flee. The volcanic matter enveloped Santorini entirely, including the town, and preserving its buildings in the process.

No human remains, however, have been excavated, and a sole gold object was found. This suggests the Minoans evacuated in an orderly manner before Thera erupted, and they had enough time to take their possessions before fleeing.

The Minoan civilization prevailed on Crete and the surrounding islands, flourishing from around 3600 BCE to 1400 BCE. Thera's eruption was credited to lead to the civilization's demise. Akrotiri was a Cretan outpost dating back to the 3rd millennium BCE. It developed gradually into one of the Aegean's urban centers and main posts.

For its time, Akrotiri was sophisticated. The town's buildings were masonry-faced and multistoried. The sophisticated drainage system was advanced, as evidenced by indoor lavatories. Akrotiri's vivid frescoes and elaborate architecture indicate a cultured settlement.

Historians and scholars believed that Akrotiri was the inspiration of Plato for Atlantis. Akrotiri can be accessed from the island's capital, Fira, and other parts of Santorini by local bus or taxi. The archaeological site was closed for a number of years for repairs. The site is now open again to visitors.

31. Areopolis, Laconia

The small town of Areopolis is considered the Greek Revolution's birthplace and is named for Ares, the Greek god of war. On May 17, 1821, revolutionary Petros Mavromichalis (Petrobey) – to defy centuries of Ottoman rule – raised the Greek flag of war.

Before it was named Areopolis early in the 20th century, it was known as Tsimova. Known as 'The Mani,' the area was home to the Maniots, a proud people led by Petrobey in the 20th century. While the revolutionary spirit was widespread in the country, the raising of the flag in that place is recorded as the first direct defiance act against the Turks. The Greek government now protects Areopolis as a historical monument.

Before it became a notable place in Greece, much of the Mani can only be accessed by sea, and pirates often invaded the Mani towns – including Areopolis. There are people that claim they can claim their lineage back to the pirates.

The town has a sense of independence. It has a church is on the main square, a central open-air market, and stone streets. Every Saturday, the market hosts a lot of local producers.

Areopolis is in Laconia, in the southwestern part of the Peloponnese Peninsula. You can reach the area from either Sparta (about 40 miles northeast) or Kalamata (about 50 miles northwest).

32. Corfu

Corfu, which is on the Ionian Sea, is the second largest of the Ionian Islands. Corfu culture is unique as, unlike the rest of the country, the island was not conquered by the Ottomans. Instead, the Venetians, the French, and the British occupied it, making the island more Western than Levantine.

In Corfu's Old Town, which is a UNESCO world heritage site, Classical, Baroque, and Renaissance 'repertoire' came to be applied successfully to artistic traditions. Fortresses, palaces, and austere

Venetian-era public buildings blend uniquely with small secluded squares and lines of washing and drying in alleyways.

To experience Corfu, some of its most beautiful walk-through spots include Spianada (the Balkans' largest square), Liston (the city's trademark), and the suburbs of Garitsa, Mandouki, and Sarokos. Other attractions include the New Fortress, the 15th century Old Fortress, and The Saint Michael and George Palace in Spianada.

Corfu is a place favored by aristocrats. The Mon Repos Palace is where Prince Philip, the future Duke of Edinburgh, was born in. Other places frequented by the aristocracy include Paleopolis and Kanoni. Achilleion – a palace built amid myrtles and cypresses – was commissioned by Empress Elisabeth of Austria as a sanctuary away from the Austrian court.

Various airlines service the island of Corfu. From the Corfu Airport, you can reach the city center by shared shuttle, taxi, or private transport. By boat, there are direct ferry links from Patra in Greece and from certain ports in Italy and Albania.

33. Crete

Crete is Greece's largest island. Here, you can marvel in old civilizations' remnants or explore impressive mountains, glorious beaches, steep gorges, and fertile valleys. You can also immerse in Crete's rich gastronomic culture.

Crete figures importantly in Greek mythology. It was in Crete that Zeus and Europa's son, Minos, was born in. King Minos made Crete into a mighty empire. The Minoan civilization, in 1450 BCE and 1400 BCE, was devastated due to the volcano Thera's eruption.

After the decline of the Minoan civilization, the Dorians settled in Crete. Other occupants included the Romans, Arabs, Venetians, and the Turks. Crete also was a Byzantine province. In 1913, Crete officially became part of Greece.

Crete's major regions include Chania, Rethymno, Heraklion, and Lasithi. Heraklion is Crete's most densely populated and largest region. The region is home to archaeological treasures, picturesque villages, vital coastal settlements, vineyards, olive groves, vast valleys, and a highly-organized tourist infrastructure.

Crete has three major airports: Nikos Kazantzakis (Heraklion), Daskalogiannis military airport (Chania), and a public airport in Sitia. From Athens, there are daily flights offered by Aegean Airlines, Athens Airways, and Olympic Air to Chania and Heraklion. Sky Express serves Sitia. If you wish to arrive in Crete by boat, you can enter through the ferry ports in Chania, Heraklion, Kastelli-Kassamos, and Sitia.

34. Mykonos

Forming part of the Cyclades, the island of Mykonos is a partygoer's paradise with its Ibiza-meets-St-Tropez vibe. In mythology, Mykonos was formed from petrified bodies of giants whom Hercules killed.

Mykonos is best known for its beaches, but Hora – the island's capital – is worth looking into. Hora is home to spectacular examples of Cycladic architecture. You can walk through the town's marble streets and be amazed at the whitewashed abodes with colorful window frames and doors.

When on the island, don't forget to sample the local Aegean cuisine. A pepper-seasoned soft cheese, kopanisti, is a Mykonos trademark. Meat lovers can enjoy louzes (pork filet cooked with spices) and sausages sprinkled with oregano and pepper. You should also not miss amigdalota, which are round cakes with rose water, caster sugar, and ground almond.

Even though it's only 10 kilometers wide and 12 to 15 kilometers long, Mykonos is one of Greece's most visited islands. Ferries and catamarans from Athens and Rafina serve the island. You can also enter Mykonos by air or by cruise ship, as the island is a favorite stop on cruise ship tours.

Taxis, small passenger boats, and buses provide transport around Mykonos, and private cars are prohibited in the towns. Summer (particularly in August) is one of Mykonos' busiest tourist periods. You can visit the island during spring or fall if you wish to avoid the crowds.

35. Rhodes

The island of Rhodes is the largest of the Dodecanese group, as well as its capital. The strategically-placed Rhodes is also historically important. The ancient city, which was built beginning 407 BC, was designed according to Hippodamus of Miletus' city planning system.

Rhodes soon became one of the eastern Mediterranean's most important trading and seafaring centers before becoming a Roman and Byzantine province. The Knights of Saint John of Jerusalem, in 1309, conquered Rhodes. They built fortifications and turned it into a multinational medieval city and administrative center. The Medieval City of Rhodes, in 1988, became a UNESCO World Heritage site.

The Old Town's highlight is The Palace of the Grand Master, a Byzantine fortress that was used by the Knights and is now a museum. The Street of the Knights is one of Europe's well-kept medieval streets. The 'new' city, which is outside the Old Town's walls, features amazing neoclassical, Venetian, and modern buildings. Some of Rhodes' Italianate-style buildings include the Post Office, Evangelismos Church, the National Theater, and the Town Hall.

Kallithea – a holiday resort strip that lines the Faliraki Beach – is on the island's east coast. Kallithea's major attractions are the long sandy beach and the Roman baths. If you want to enjoy natural treks, head to the Rhodes' southern coast. The island's southernmost tip is popular for kitesurfing and windsurfing. Walk along the old paths and discover shady woods, golden fields, and gentle valleys and hills.

You can enter Rhodes by plane or by ship. There are flights from Thessaloniki and Athens. Rhodes' port has connections to the Piraeus port. The 12-hour trip has stops at the islands of Leros, Patmos, Kos, and Kalymnos. Rhodes is also connected to Crete and the other Dodecanese islands.

36. Symi Harbor, Rhodes

The small island of Symi – with a population of about 2,500 – is known for its harbor, which is considered the most beautiful in Greece.

In the 19th century, the sponge trade made the town rich. Boats sailed as far as the North African coast, and the sponge fishermen were away from their beloved home for a long time. There are still sponges sold locally. However, the products are mostly imported.

Symi Harbor is a protected area, as most of the buildings date back to the 19th century and are Neoclassical in design. If you want to stay away from tourist areas, you can climb the Yialos stairs. Walkers would surely be delighted with the island's landscape, especially during late summer or spring when the temperature is mild. Although rewarding, certain terrains in the island can be tough.

You can only travel by catamaran or ferry from Rhodes if you want to reach Symi Harbor. After reaching the harbor, visitors normally take a lengthy trip along the Turkish coast and then travel around the island's uninhabited coast before visitors stumble on the hill-lined, small inlet with its neo-classical, pastel-colored homes.

You can get around in Symi by bus. The service runs back and forth from Pedi to Yialos passing through Chorio throughout the day and until nighttime.

37. Vatheia, Laconia

The mostly-abandoned town of Vatheia in Laconia rests atop a mountainous rise in the Mani Peninsula landscape. The tower houses are the norm in the region, where bloody and lengthy feuds often occurred between clan and family groups. Built during the 18th and 19th centuries, Vatheia contains some of the region's most striking tower clusters.

A travel writer, Patrick Leigh Fermor, had written of Vatheia. He wrote of a wide jagged ridge with broken towers like an iguana's spikes. An angular collection of towers was rooted in a cloud of olive and cactus, ending on the edge of the ledges' steep fall.

During the 1980s, there was an attempt to convert Vatheia into a functional tourist shop, with amenities and hotels. The efforts were unsuccessful, and the town remains un-renovated and nearly uninhabited. The town square, which is surrounded by towers, is quiet, cool, and home to a tiny church. Some of the towers have holes or have disintegrated due to vegetation overgrowth.

By 2011, only 33 people lived in the nearly abandoned town. It's not exactly a ghost town, but it's still a haunting and lonely place to explore.

If you are already in the Mani Peninsula, it's easy to travel to Vatheia by car, and the town makes for an excellent spot on a hike or day trip. You may want to bring along lunch, a snack, and water, but there are a few restaurants and grocery stores nearby. As the slope is somewhat steep, it's a good idea to wear sturdy yet comfortable shoes.

Chapter 6: Amazing Museums

38. Archaeological Museum of Thessaloniki

The Archaeological Museum of Thessaloniki guides you through a trip of Greek Macedonia's history. Some of the museum exhibits include those of Prehistoric Macedonia and 7th century BCE Macedonia until late antiquity. You get to know more about the politics, economy, religion, social organization, everyday life, and art from the Archaic times to the Roman period.

Know more about the Metropolis of Macedonia – Thessaloniki – as well as the open-air exhibit of the museum. Walk through funerary monuments like the altars and sarcophagus found in the eastern and western cemetery of Thessaloniki. Visit a reconstructed Roman residence with authentic mosaic floors.

The museum's most impressive exhibit is the Gold of Macedon. The bronze Derveti krater depicts Dionysus and Ariadne's sacred wedding. While it may look golden, it's actually made of tin and copper.

The Archaeological Museum of Thessaloniki is located at 6 Manoli Adronikou Street in a modernist building designed by Patroklos Karandinos. The building is 10 minutes from Aristotelous Square. When going there by bus, you can use the 'cultural route' 50. You can use lines 7, 10, 11, 12, 31, 39, or 58. When you have enjoyed your fill of Macedonian history, you can sip coffee under the trees at the museum café, which is next to the sculptures patio.

39. Entomological Museum of Volos, Thessaly

The Entomological Museum of Volos may only be as large as several rooms, but it's more than just a work of preservation. Doctor Athanasios Koutroumpas' collection is growing, with new species constantly added to enrich its extant specimens' context. Presently, the museum has 35,000 various insects from different species, with many of such species considered unique.

The museum is more densely populated by various butterfly specimens, numbering to over 10,000 species, genus, and subspecies. The insect specimens are arranged precisely and classified according to International Statistical Entomology rules. One of the specimens is native only to South America, the Thysania Agrippina, which is deemed the world's largest butterfly due to its 40-centimeter wingspan.

Coming from various parts of Europe and Greece, and enriched by specimens from all over the world, the displayed species were gathered by Koutroumpas during his trips or were donated by international colleagues.

The Entomological Museum of Volos is located at Zachos and General Makriyannis Streets. Athanasios Koutroumpas conducts the tour, and museum entrance is free. To visit the museum, you may call (+030) 24210.48.556, 60.601. You also need to book an appointment.

40. Goulandris Museum of Cycladic Art, Athens

Established in 1986, the Goulandris Museum of Cycladic Art is dedicated to the promotion and study of ancient cultures of Cyprus and the Aegean, with emphasis on the 3rd millennium BCE's Cycladic Art. In the 1960s, Nicholas and

Dolly Goulandris started collecting artifacts after the Greek state allowed them to. The Goulandris collection, recognized quickly by the region's scholars, focused on marble vessels and figurines.

The Goulandris collection, which was initially presented in 1978 to the Benaki Museum, sought its own museum a decade and a half after the Goulandris couple began to accumulate. Years after visiting the Benaki, the collection traveled to major museums and galleries worldwide. After the collection has made its round worldwide, the Museum of Cycladic Art – in January 1986 – was inaugurated.

Built in central Athens in 1985, the Museum's main building was designed by Greek architect Ioannis Vikelas. The Museum, in 1991, acquired a new wing – the Stathatos Mansion – at the corner of Herodotou Street and Vassilissis Sofias Avenue. The main building is located at Neophytou Douka 4, Athens.

The Goulandris Museum of Art, which is one of the city's great museums, has over 200 objects. A museum shop on the site has ancient art books and reproductions of collection items.

41. Heraklion Archaeological Museum, Crete

The Heraklion Archaeological Museum is one of Greece's most important museums. Located in the town center, the Museum was constructed from 1937 to 1940 on a site occupied previously by the Roman Catholic Saint-Francis Monastery, which was destroyed in 1856 during an earthquake.

Built to withstand strong seismic activity, the Museum – designed by Patroklos Karantinos – is a vital modernist architectural example and was commended by Bauhaus. The construction materials – like the polychrome veined marble – and colors remind of several Minoan wall paintings that imitate the revetment of marble.

The Museum contains artifacts from Cretan prehistory and later history, covering about 5,500 years from the Neolithic to the Roman periods. The important Minoan collection contains unique Minoan art examples. The Museum has 27 galleries, modern laboratories, an audio-visual display gallery, a cafeteria, a cloakroom, and a museum shop that sells books, museum copies, slides, and postcards.

The Heraklion Archaeological Museum is a Ministry of Culture designated Special Regional Service, of which its purpose is to safeguard, acquire, record, conserve, publish, study, promote, and display Cretan artifacts from the Prehistoric period to the Late Roman period. The Museum arranges temporary exhibits internationally and locally, hosts various cultural events, and collaborates with scholarly and scientific institutions.

42. Komboloi Museum, Argolis

If you are fascinated with beads of all kinds, a trip to the Komboloi Museum in Nafplio, Argolis should be on your itinerary. Aris and Rallou Evangelinos, in 1963, started to be interested in komboloi, which are small strings threaded with stones. Komboloi is more secular in nature, and are used for stress relief; thus, the alternate term – worry beads.

In a historical context, strings of beads methodically handled are thought to calm the spirit and the mind. The Buddhist japa mala and the Catholic rosaries are examples of beaded strings. The komboloi, however, are not used in a religious capacity.

In 1998, the Evangelinos opened the Komboloi Museum (Greek Worry Bead Museum) dedicated to their interest in komboloi. On the ground floor, there's a workshop for crafting komboloi and refurbishing crumbling komboloi. The upper floor features worry beads from various religions

(Buddhism, Hinduism, Christianity, and Islam) and trace the beads' history.

The Greek komboloi constitutes the largest collection. The komboloi vary in material and length, but they are normally made from coral or amber, as the stones are said to feel best. The museum shop sells komboloi for the weary traveler.

The Greek Folk Art Museum is nearby. Other places of interest in the Nafplio area are St. Spyridon Church, The War Museum, Frangokklisia, and The Peloponnesian Folklore Foundation Museum.

43. Museum of Byzantine Culture, Thessaloniki

The Museum of Byzantine Culture in Thessaloniki is a tribute to the city's Byzantine beauty and character. Historically, Thessaloniki – together with Constantinople – was once a 'co-reigning' city of the Byzantine Empire.

Built in 1994, the Museum is housed in a contemporary facility that includes well-organized, advanced conservation storerooms and laboratories. Hundreds of unique artifacts and exhibits through the Byzantine period are displayed in various rooms.

The Museum is a window into Thessaloniki's Byzantine past and is classified into thematic collections and sections. Wall paintings and mosaics, Byzantine religious architecture and icons, rare books, scripts, and jewelry await the visitor. The Museum has a small amphitheater, a café, and an outdoor section to hold exhibitions are some of the extra features for Museum visitors. As one of Greek public architecture's best examples, the Museum integrates successfully contemporary elements and Greece's public heritage.

The Museum of Byzantine Culture is located in 2, Stratou Ave., GR 54013, Thessaloniki. During summers, it opens from 12:30 pm to 7:30 pm on

Mondays, and from 8:00 am to 7:00 pm from Tuesdays to Sundays. During winters, it opens from 10:30 am to 5:00 pm on Mondays, 8:00 am to 5:00 pm from Tuesdays to Fridays, and 8:00 am to 7:00 pm on Saturdays and Sundays.

44. National Archaeological Museum, Athens

The National Archaeological Museum in Athens is one of Greece's largest museums. While it was originally intended to secure archaeological finds from 19th century excavations in and around the city, it slowly became the country's main museum and was enriched with ancient treasures from all over the country.

The Museum is within the 19th century Neoclassical building designed by L. Lange and renovated by Ernst Ziller. The Museum's more than 20,000 exhibits provide a glimpse into Greek civilization from Prehistory to Late Roman Antiquity.

The Museum's exhibition space encompasses a total area of 8,000 square meters. The five main permanent collections include:

- The Prehistoric Collection
- The Sculptures Collection
- The Vase and Minor Objects Collection
- The Metallurgy Collection and
- The Egyptian and Near East Antiquities Collection.

The Museum also has a library with rare publications and a photographic archive. There also are modern conservation laboratories for pottery, metal, organic materials, and stone. Also, there are a chemistry laboratory, a photographic laboratory, and a cast workshop.

The Museum has a standard EUR7 entrance fee, which is reduced to EUR3 for EU senior citizens and students from non-EU countries. Opening hours are from 1:00 pm to 8:00 pm on Mondays, 8:00 am to 8:00 pm from Tuesdays to Saturdays, and 8:00 am to 3:00 pm on Sundays and public holidays.

45. Palace of the Grand Master, Rhodes

The Palace of the Grand Master, which is built at Rhodes' medieval city's highest point, is located at the end of the Street of the Knights. Originally built on the Temple of the Sun God's foundations, the palace used to be the governor's residence. The palace also was the city of Rhodes' administrative center.

The Knights of Saint John built the palace in the 14th century and is characterized by its arched gate and spherical towers. The massive palace used to have 158 rooms, but only 24 rooms are open to visitors nowadays. The rooms contain 16th and 17th century furniture, sculptures, multi-colored marbles, fine Oriental vases, and carpets.

The frescoes of artists like F. Vellan and P. Gaudenzi are of special importance, as are the floors with a mosaic of Byzantine and ancient Roman art. Moreover, the interior yard is adorned with Greek and Roman period statues.

In 1856, the palace was substantially destroyed by explosives that were hidden in the church of Saint John's basement. During the turn of the 20th century, the Italians restored the palace. The palace also served as a holiday residence for notables like Benito Mussolini and King Victor Emmanuel III.

Now a museum, the palace is owned by the Greek State. Various performances and exhibitions take place in the rooms of the palace. The Palace of the Grand Master is located at Odos Ippoton, Rhodes

85100, and is open from 8:00 am to 4:00 pm from Tuesdays to Sundays.

Chapter 7: Amazing Natural Wonders

46. Cape Matapan Caves, Laconia

Also known as Cape Taenaron, Cape Matapan is a landmass at the Mani Peninsula. It separates the Messenian Gulf to the west and the Laconian Gulf to the east. In mythology, the cape is a backdrop for various important stories. The ancient Greeks held the belief that caves on the cape's tip were entrances to the underworld – Hades.

In the stories, the caves are where Orpheus entered Hades in search of Eurydice. When Hercules entered the underworld, he entered through the caves. The caves are not only significant in myths. The Spartans revered the caves as a place of worship. Along the rocky headland, the Spartans built temples to their deities. One of these is the Temple of Poseidon.

During the Byzantine times, the temple began to be used as a Christian church – even up to today.

The Cape Matapan Caves feature a complex tapestry of stalagmites and stalactites. While the natural formations are partly submerged, the caverns can be explored by boat.

Mani Peninsula is a unique tourist attraction, and it takes an adventurous soul to go there. The region doesn't have a premier public transportation system, as there are not many people living in the area. If you wish to visit the legendary underworld, you have to bring your own transportation. It's also important to fill up the tank at the gas station closest to the region.

47. Kastania's Cave, Voies, Peloponnese

Kastania's Cave used to be hidden to the world until Kostas Stivaktas – at the turn of the 20th century – broke open a small fissure when he noticed bees entering and leaving it. The bees emerged seemingly refreshed. Upon breaking the crack, Stivaktas saw a rare and beautiful cave full of stalagmites and stalactites in extraordinary shapes and colors.

Stivaktas and his descendants, since then, have been visiting the cave and get water from the cave's well. In 1958, the cave was assigned protection by Kastania's community. The cave, which is densely-packed, is now open for tours.

Kastania's Cave houses unique rock arrangements that took 3 million years to form. Formations like level stalagmites and disks have formed along the ceilings and walls. Aside from the rock formations, cave visitors can see the resident creature – the 'dolichopodo,' which is an insect that resembles a locust and is both deaf and blind.

Kastania's Cave is located in the town of Voies, which is part of the Monemvasia municipality in Peloponnese.

48. Lemnos Sand Dunes, Lemnos

The Lemnos Sand Dunes are nestled within the Lemnos desert and is an oddity in a mostly-green island. With the wind, the 17-acre desert constantly changes in dimension and shape. The winds can also create majestic sand dunes that are known locally as 'pacchies ammoudies' (thick sands).

While seemingly a barren landscape, the dunes actually host local fauna like white rabbits. Moreover, white lilies grow from the dunes, while olive trees surround the desert's edge. When you walk through the forest to the scorching desert, you may feel you're in an ethereal fantasy. Because of Lemnos' unique terrain – with its varying landscape – several film directors have shot their respective movies' desert scenes on the island.

To reach the Lemnos Sand Dunes comfortably, you may need a four-wheel-drive vehicle, as the dunes can be accessed only by a dirt road. On hot days, don't visit at noon, as the sand can be excruciatingly hot. To experience the dunes, it's best to visit the site before sunset or early in the morning.

49. Olive Tree of Vouves, Ano Vouves, Crete

You may wonder why an olive tree is specially mentioned here. The Olive Tree of Vouves is Greece's oldest olive tree and has been bearing fruit even after 2,000 years. An indication of the tree's age is the fact that two Geometric Period (900 BCE to 700 BCE) cemeteries were found nearby.

Despite being old, the tree still produces olives. A museum stands next to the olive tree to celebrate Greece and the Mediterranean's olive tradition. It has been evident that Greek olive cultivation has been around since the Neolithic period. There are references to olive products in the writings of

Pliny the Elder, Herodotus, and the Hebrew accounts of the Exodus.

The olive tree, with a width of 15 feet, has been around during the time of Muhammad and Jesus Christ, of the Bubonic Plague, and when Beethoven composed the 5th, among other events. Arguably, the Olive Tree of Vouves is Greece's most important tree. Its importance was exemplified during the 2004 Athens Olympics and the 2008 Beijing Olympics when laurels were crafted from the Vouves tree's branches.

The Olive Tree of Vouves is located in the town of Kolymvari, which is located in the northwestern portion of Crete.

50. Sami, Cephalonia

Nestled on the island of Cephalonia, the largest of Western Greece's Ionian Islands, Sami has two amazing geological features: the Melissani Lake and Drogarati Cave. The distance between the two features is short that you can visit these two wonders in only a day.

The Drogarati Cave was discovered 300 years ago after an earthquake opened up an entrance that was closed previously. It was only in 1963, though, that the public had access to the cave. Adventurous visitors are treated with the cave's beautiful stalactites and stalagmites. The 'Sala of

Apotheosis' – the cave's largest room – is illuminated and measures 900 square meters. Due to its spectacular acoustics, the room is often used for concerts.

Lake Melissani was named after excavations in 1951, and 1962 revealed Minoan depictions of the god Pan and the nymph Melissanthi. Many years ago, the lake was created when a massive cavern collapsed, leaving an opening to the surface. On sunny days from 11 am to 1 pm, the lake is an ethereal blue.

You can enter Cephalonia by air and by ferry. Kefalonia International Airport is located near Lassi and Argostoli, and flights to the mainland are provided by Olympic Air and Sky Express. Ferries from Italy and the Greek mainland and its islands also serve Cephalonia and Sami.

51. Volcanic Rocks of Lemnos, Lemnos

The island of Lemnos is the mythical location of the forge of Hephaestus, the god of fire, metallurgy, and blacksmiths. Hephaestus, according to legend, landed in Lemnos after Zeus threw him off Mount Olympus. Because of Lemnos' volcanic nature, it's attributed to Hephaestus.

The long-extinct Miocene volcanoes that had spewed lava on the Lemnos shores have left behind entrancing and peculiar rock formations. The locals call them 'fragokefala' or 'faraklo' – 'bald heads' or 'bald,' which refers to the tawny orbs and barren hills that grace the landscape. The hardened lava is frozen in various bizarre shapes, from rock face ripples to built-up three-dimensional spirals.

The Volcanic Rocks of Lemnos are on a site at the island's north edge. It's beyond the Neolithic settlement of Poliochni. Gravel paths lead from the town to the Aegean. While it may be moments before finding the right path, the rugged Lemnos coastline is worth the experience. The Volcanic Rocks of Lemnos are located after the village of Propouli. A detour is off the road, and you can see the rocks beside the beach.

In Lemnos, the airport and the Myrina port serve the island's transportation needs. Ferry routes and flights often change, and peak during summer. There are one or two flights a day, usually from Athens.

Other Books by Publisher

For more travel guides by 51 Amazing Things, go to:

amzn.to/2vkVdxp

Made in the USA
Middletown, DE
09 December 2017